A Father To His Freshman Son: A Father To His Graduate Girl

Edward Sandford Martin

In the interest of creating a more extensive selection of rare historical book reprints, we have chosen to reproduce this title even though it may possibly have occasional imperfections such as missing and blurred pages, missing text, poor pictures, markings, dark backgrounds and other reproduction issues beyond our control. Because this work is culturally important, we have made it available as a part of our commitment to protecting, preserving and promoting the world's literature. Thank you for your understanding.

ATLANTIC READINGS
Number 5

A FATHER TO HIS FRESHMAN SON
A FATHER TO HIS GRADUATE GIRL

BY

EDWARD SANFORD MARTIN

UNIV. OF
CALIFORNIA

The Atlantic Monthly Press, Inc.
BOSTON

A Father to his Freshman Son

By Edward Sanford Martin

No doubt, my son, you have got out of me already what there was to help or mar you. You are eighteen years old and have been getting it, more or less and off and on, for at least seventeen of those years. I regret the imperfections of the source. No doubt you have recognized them. To have a father who is attentive to the world, indulgent to the flesh, and with a sort of kindness for the Devil — dear son, it is a good deal of a handicap! Be sure I make allowances for you because of it. *Ex eo fonte* — *fons*, masculine, as I remember; *fons* and *mons* and *pons*, and one other. Should the pronoun be *illo?* As you know, I never was an accurate scholar, and I suppose you're not — *Ex eo fonte* the stream is bound to run not quite clear.

My advice to you is quite likely to be bad, partly from the imperfection of its source, partly because I am not you, and partly because of my imperfect acquaintance with the conditions you are about to meet. When I came to college my father gave me no advice. He gave me his love and some necessary money, which did not come, I fear, as easy as the love. His venerable uncle who lived with us — my great uncle — gave me his blessing and told me, I remember, that so far as book-learning went, I could learn as much without going to college. Still he did not discourage my going. He was quite right. I could have got more book-learning out of college than I did get in college, and I suppose that you, too, might get, out, more than you will get, in. Of course, that's not the whole story; neither is it true of all people. For me, college abounded in distractions, and I suppose it will for you. And I was incorrigibly sociable and ready to spend time to get acquainted, and more, to stay acquainted, and if you have that propensity you need n't think it was left on the doorstep. You come by it lawfully. Getting acquainted is, for most of us, one of the important branches. But it's only one of them, and to devote one's whole time to it is a mistake, and one that the dean will help you avoid if necessary, which probably, if I know you at all, it won't be.

It is important to know people, but it is more important to be worth knowing. College offers you at least two valuable details of opportunity: a large variety of people to know, and a large variety of means to make yourself better worth knowing. I hope, my son, that you will avail yourself of both these details.

This is a mechanical age, and the most obtrusive of

A Father to his Freshman Son

the current mechanisms is the automobile. It has valves and cylinders and those things that give it power and speed, and rubber tires that it runs on, and a wheel and steering-gear and handles and treadles by which it is directed. Your body, especially your stomach, is the rubber tires; your brains are the cylinders and valves; and your will and the spiritual part of you are the chauffeur and his wheel.

I beg you to be kind to your stomach, as heretofore. It needs no alcohol at your time of life — if ever — and the less you find occasion to feed into it, the more prosperous both your physical and mental conditions are likely to be. I am aware that life, and college life in particular, has its convivial intervals; but you might as well understand (and I have been remiss, or have wasted time, if you do not understand it already) that alcohol is one of the chief man-traps, abounding in mischiefs if you play with it too hard. Be wary, always wary, with it, my son, and especially with hard liquor.

Your mind, like your body, is a thing whereof the powers are developed by effort. That is a principal use, as I see it, of hard work in studies. Unless you train your body you can't be an athlete, and unless you train your mind you can't be much of a scholar. The four miles an oarsman covers at top speed is in itself nothing to the good, but the physical capacity to hold out over the course is thought to be of some worth. So a good part of what you learn by hard study may not be permanently retained, and may not seem to be of much final value, but your mind is a better and more powerful instrument because you have learned it. 'Knowledge is power,' but still more the faculty of acquiring and using knowledge is power. If you have a trained and powerful mind, you are bound to have stored it with something, but its value is more in what it can do, what it can grasp and use, than in what it contains; and if it were possible, as it is not, to come out of college with a trained and disciplined mind and nothing useful in it, you would still be ahead, and still, in a manner, educated. Think of your mind as a muscle to be developed; think of it as a searchlight that is to reveal the truth to you, and don't cheat it or neglect it.

As to competitive scholarship, to my mind it is like competitive athletics, — good for those who have the powers and like the game. Tests are useful; they stimulate one's ambition, and so do competitions. But a success in competitive scholarship, like a success in competitive athletics, may, of course, be too dearly bought. Not by you, though, I surmise, my son. If you were more urgent, either as a scholar or as an athlete, I might think it needful to warn you not to wear your tires out scorching too early in life. As things are, I say to you, as I often say to myself: Don't dawdle; don't scramble. When you work, work;

A Father to his Freshman Son

when you play, play; when you rest, rest; and think all the time.

When you get hold of an instructor who is worth attention, give him attention. That is one way of getting the best that a college has to offer. A great deal you may get from books, but some of the most valuable things are passed from mind to mind, and can only be had from some one who has them, or else from the great Source of all truth. I suspect that the subtle development we call 'culture' is one of those things, and the great spiritual valuables are apt to come that way.

You know you are still growing, both in mind and body, and will continue so to be for years to come, — I hope, always. One of the valuable things about college is that it gives you time to grow. You won't have to earn any money and will have time to think and get acquainted with yourself and others, as well as with some of the wisdom that is spread upon the records. You would be so engaged, more or less, in these years, wherever you might be. But in college, where you are so much your own man, and are freed from the demands and solicitudes of your parents, the conditions for it are exceptionally favorable. I suppose that is one thing that continues the colleges in business, since I read so often that at present they are entirely misdirected and teach the wrong things in the wrong way.

But nobody denies that they give the young a breathing spell. Breathe, my son; breathe freely. Remember that the aim of all these prospective processes is to bring out the man there is in you, and arm him more or less for the jousts ahead. It is not to make you over into somebody else: that can't be done, — not in three or four years, anyhow; but only to bring out, and train as much as possible of you. There's plenty in most of us if we can only get it out; more, very much more, than we ever do get out. So will you please think of college as a nursery in which you are to grow a while, — and mind you do grow, — and then, presently, to be transplanted. It is not as if college was the chief arena of human effort. Nevertheless, for your effort, while you are there, it is the chief arena, and I am far from giving you the counsel to put off trying until you leave.

I hear a good deal about clubs and societies: how many there are, how important they are; how it is that, if a youth shall gain the whole of scholarship and all athletics and not 'make' a proper club, he shall still fall something short of success in college. Parents I meet who are more concerned about clubs than about either scholarship or deportment. They are concerned and at the same time bothered: so many strategies and chances the clubs involve; so bad it may be to be in this one; so bad to be out of that; so much choice there is between them, and so much choice

A Father to his Freshman Son

exercised within them, by which any mother's hopeful may be excluded.

There is a democratic ideal of a great college without any clubs, where the lion and the lamb shall escort one another about with tails entwined, and every student shall be like every other student, and have similar habits and associates. This ideal is a good deal discussed and a good deal applauded in the public press. Whether it will ever come true I can't tell, but there has been some form or other of clubs in our older colleges, I suppose, for one or two centuries, and they are there now and will at least last out your time; so it may be you will have to take thought about them in due time.

Not much, however, until they take thought of you.

You see, clubs seem to be a sort of natural provision, just as tails were, maybe, before humanity outgrew them. I guess there is a propensity of nature toward groups, and the natural basis of grouping seems to be likeness in feathers and habits. The propensity works to include the like and, incidentally but necessarily, to exclude the unlike. Whether it is the Knights of the Round Table or the Knights of the Garter or the Phi Beta Kappa, you see these principles working. The measure of success in a club is its ability to make people want to join it, and that seems to be best demonstrated and preserved by keeping most of them out.

Now the advantages of the clubs are considerable.

To have a place always open where you can hang up your hat, and where a hospitable welcome always awaits you, and where there is enough of a crowd and not too much, and where you can in your later years inspect at all times a family of selected undergraduates, — all that is valuable and good, and pleasant besides, and this continuity of interest that the clubs foster among their members helps to keep up in those members a lively and helpful interest in their college. The drawback to the clubs is their essential selfishness, and their disposition to take you out of a large family and limit you to a small one, and one that is not yours by birth, or entirely by choice, but is selected for you largely by other persons.

In any club you yield a certain amount of freedom and individuality, the amount being determined by the degree in which the club absorbs you. Don't yield too much! Don't take the mould of any club! A college is always bigger than its clubs, and the biggest thing in a college is always a man. The object of being in college is to develop as a man. If clubs help in that development, — and I think they do help some men, — they are a gain; but, of course, if they dwarf you down to the dimensions of a club-man, they are a loss. Some men take their club shape, such as it is, and find a sufficient satisfaction in it. Others react on their clubs, take what they have to give, add to it what is to be had elsewhere, and turn out rather more

A Father to his Freshman Son

valuable people than if they had had no club experience.

At all events, don't take this matter of the clubs too hard. For those youths, comparatively few, who by luck and circumstances find themselves eligible to them, they are an interesting form of discipline or indulgence, and I will not say that they are unimportant. Neither would I have you keep out of them because of their drawbacks. If you begin by keeping out of all things that have drawbacks, your progress in this world will involve constant hesitations. Alcohol has numerous drawbacks, but I don't advise you to be a teetotaller. Tobacco has drawbacks, but I believe you smoke it. Money has drawbacks, and so has advertisement. But, bless you, we have to take things as they come and deal with them as we can. The trick is to get the kernel and eliminate the shuck. A large proportion of people do the opposite. If you can manage that way with the clubs, — provided you ever get a chance, — you will be amused to observe in due time how large a proportion of your brethren value these organizations chiefly for their shuck, and grasp most eagerly at that. For the shuck, as I see it, is exclusiveness, which is not valuable except to persons justly doubtful of their own merits. Whereas the kernel is the fellowship of like minds which has always been treasured by the wise.

The clubs, my son, some more than others, are recruited considerably from what is known as the leisure class. To be sure, I don't see any very definite or important leisure class about in our land. Everybody who amounts to anything works, and always did and must, for you can't amount to anything otherwise; but the people who have money laid up ahead for them, are apt to work somewhat less strenuously than the rest of us, and not so much for money. Don't get it into your head that you want to tie up to the leisure class, or that the condition of not having to work is desirable. Have it in mind that you are to work just about as hard as the quality of your tires and cylinders will warrant. Plan to get into the game if you have to go on your hands and knees. Plan to earn your living somehow. Don't aim to go through life spoon-fed; don't aim to get a soft seat. If you do, you won't have your fair share of fun. There is no real fun in ease, except as you need it because you have worked hard.

I say, plan to earn your living! Whether you actually earn the money you live on, makes no great difference, though in your case I guess you'll have to if you are going to live at all well. But if you get money without earning it, it leaves you in debt to society. Somebody has to earn the money you spend. In mine, factory, railroad, or office, somebody works for the money that supports you. No matter where the money comes from, that is true: somebody has to earn

A Father to his Freshman Son

it. If you get it without due labor of your own, you owe for it. Recognize that debt and qualify yourself to discharge it. Study to put back into the world somewhat more than you take out of it. Study to be somewhat more than merely worth your keep. Study to shoulder the biggest load your strength can carry. That is life. That is the great sport that brings the great compensations to the soul. Getting regular meals and nice clothes, and acceptable shelter and transportation, and agreeable acquaintances, is only a means to an end, and if you accept the means and shirk the end, the means will pall on you.

I said 'agreeable acquaintances.' A very large proportion of the acquaintances you can make will be agreeable if you can bring enough knowledge and a sufficiently hospitable spirit to your relations with them. I don't counsel you to cultivate the arts of popularity, for they are apt not to wash, — apt, that is, to conflict with inside qualities that are vastly more valuable than they are. But keep, in so far as you can, an open heart. There is no one to whom you are not related if only you can find the relation; there is no one but you owe him a benefit if you can see one you can do him.

Don't be too nice. It is such an impediment to usefulness as stuttering is to speech, — a sort of spiritual indigestion; a hesitation in your carbureter. By all means, be a gentleman, in manners and spirit, in so far as you know how, but be one from the inside out.

If you had come as far as you have in life without acquiring manners, you might well blush for your parents and teachers. I don't think you have, but I beg you hold on to all the good manners you have, and get more. Good manners seem to me a good deal to seek among present-day youth, but I suppose they have always been fairly scarce, and the more appreciated for their scarcity. Tobacco manners are uncommonly free and bad in this generation; more so, I think, than they were in mine. Since cigarettes came in, especially, youths seem to feel licensed to smoke them in all places and company. And the boys are prone to too much ease of attitude, and lounge and loll appallingly in company, and I see them in parlors with their legs crossed in such a fashion that their feet might almost as well be in the ladies' laps.

Have a care for these matters of deportment. Be strict with yourself and your postures. Keep your legs and feet where they belong; they were not meant for parlor ornaments. Show respect for people! Lord bless me! the things I see done by males with a claim to be gentlemen: tobacco-smoke puffed in women's faces; men who ought to know better, smoking as they drive out with ladies; men who put their feet on the table and expect you to talk over them! Show respect for people; for all kinds of people, including yourself, for

A Father to his Freshman Son

self-respect is at the bottom of all good manners. They are the expression of discipline, of good-will, of respect for other people's rights and comfort and feelings. I suppose good manners are unselfish, but the most selfish people might well cultivate them, they are so remunerative. In the details of life, in the public vehicles, in crowds, and in all situations where the demand presses hard on supply, what you get by hogging is incomparably less than what you get by courtesy. The things you must scramble and elbow for are not worth having; not one of them. They are the swill of life, my son; leave them to swine.

You will have to think more or less about yourself, because that belongs to your time of life, provided you are the sort that thinks at all. But don't overdo it. You won't, because you will find it, as all healthy people do, a subject in which over-indulgence tends rapidly to nausea. To have one's self always on one's mind is to lodge a kill-joy; to act always from calculation is a sure path to blunders.

Most of these specific counsels I set down more for your entertainment than truly to guide you. You don't live by maxims any more than you speak by rules of grammar. You will speak by ear (improving, I hope, in your college environment), and you will live by whatever light there is in you, getting more, I hope, as you go along.

Grow in grace, my son! If your spirit is right, the

details of life will take care of their own adjustment. Go to church; if not invariably, then variably. They don't require it any more in college, but you can't afford not to; for the churches reflect and recall — very imperfectly, to be sure — the religion and the spirit of Christ; and on that the whole of our civilization rests. Get understanding of that. It is by far the most important knowledge in the whole book, the great fountain of sanity, tolerance, and political and social wisdom, a gateway to all kinds of truth, a rectifying and consoling current through all of life.

A Father to his Graduate Girl
By Edward S. Martin

For you, my daughter in cap and gown, the reflections that greeted your graduation in white muslin only four years ago will have to be revised. All the wisdom of the ages could be drawn upon for admonition, as the ministrations of the Miss Minervas culminated on that June morning, and you made your curtsy to the world that was. You cast about for a year, inspecting the show to which you had gained admission; and then, as you remember, having stronger aspirations for knowledge than for social exercises, you went to college. Here you are, again inspecting the planet you were born into, and looking, I suppose, for a suitable place to take hold of its activities.

But bless me! what a distracted tragedy of a planet! All the people in it running about like ants in an ant-hill that the ploughshare has cut through; every tradition upset; every habit of life threatened with disturbance! Here you come, bringing a new education to a new heaven and a new earth! Take your parent by the hand, my dear, and lead him forth into the unknown. This is no world of his. Yours it may be; yours it must be, as much as any one's; yours to make and shape, and share its destinies. I see not much further into it than that it must have work for such as you; and as always heretofore you have done the task that you attempted, I have the more faith to find you equal to whatever tasks are coming.

Of what you have learned in these three scholastic years now crowned with A.B., I have only vague and general knowledge, but I know that you have partaken faithfully of the repast that was set before you, and that, if there is anything good for girls in a college education, you must have got it. I can get assurance from expert educators that you have been taught nothing by the right method, and little or nothing that you should have learned, and that you face life again not really much to the good for all your recent endeavors. But that I shall not believe. Between ideal education and what you have obtained, no doubt a great gulf stretches; but at least you have got your share of what has been offered to your generation, and I own that I look upon your bachelor of arts degree as a life-belt strapped around you as you stand on the deck of a ship that navigates a zone of danger. If it is any good for a girl to have practiced a little to live her own life, to choose her own companions, to form her own opinions and test them for herself, surely this is the time and this the state of the world for that good to become apparent.

I notice that this distinction seems to rule between the girls who come out of boarding-schools and you beginning Bachelors: that they look forward to a little play-time period, and that most of you look for 'a job.' The difference does not go so deep as appears, for both of you are after training, with a view to future employment, and are likely in the end to come to similar activities. For women are women, and will be to the end; and the work they do, in the long run and with due exceptions, will be women's work. The boarding-school misses are quite as apt to pick up valuable lessons in applied energy in their playtime, as you will be in the employment that you hope to find.

At least, I suppose that you hope to find it. All the graduating college girls, having had a training and learned something, — at least, they hope so, — want to try it out on real work and find out what it is good for. Certainly this is their year if there ever was one. The young men graduates of colleges in '61 found the Civil War ready made for them, and most of them, deferring all other occupations, went into it. Here's a war ready for you, and one that promises to have a job waiting for every woman that is ready for it. It may be a job that women have been used to do; it may be something quite novel and untried. If the latter, so much the better for you whose training is believed to have made you a little readier than your sisters to try out experiments. A little more than other girls, the girls who have been to college are used to variety of association. They are apt, not only to know more girls than their boarding-school sisters, but more kinds of girls. In some of the big girls' colleges in the great cities there is obtainable an experience of human fellowship something like that which imaginative persons see as one of the precious possibilities of universal military service. If the dog-tent sheltering two young citizens from widely different social layers is an instrument of democracy, so is the classroom bench of a big girls' college in a great city.

Three years ago we thought that employments for women had been marvelously amplified, and so they had. The girls had flocked into offices; they were typewriters and stenographers, lawyers, doctors, editors, cashiers and bookkeepers; they did most of the work of the great department stores; they were deep in social service, and had almost monopolized the great profession of teaching. But since the war began, and men by the million have been called into it, armies of women almost equally large have been poured into the places these men left vacant. In Europe before the war women contended for employment; but since the war began, almost all employments, except actual military service, have contended for the women. Women censor the mails; women make the munitions; women,

A Father to his Graduate Girl

even in England, tend the cattle and till the land. Only by this vast, wholesale coöperation of the women of the nations with the men of the nations has the war been kept going. Whenever there was work to be done and lack of men to do it, women have been enlisted.

And that, my daughter with your sheepskin in your hand, is the world into which you have graduated. It is a world in crisis; a world struggling toward a salvation only to be won by bitter effort; a world to which these states have suddenly been joined again after four generations of separation. Physically we Americans are far distant from the war and its agonies, but spiritually, mentally, nationally, it has become our affair and we are joined to it. It is our concern now that it shall come out right and do its appointed work of destruction and renovation. Our great estate and all our powers are committed to that vast duty. No one of us is exempt from contributing what we have and what we are to that endeavor.

The deep impressions which affect our lives are apt to come suddenly, to be matters of weeks or months of very active thought, rather than of years of slow experience. Like enough you, my daughter, and your coevals, will have your ideas about many important matters shaped by the thoughts that are born of this crisis in human affairs. No one who is really alive will escape those thoughts. They will concern the relations of nations and of all the people who compose them. One of the great lessons that the war is teaching is the power and duty of coöperation; that no one may live for self alone, but each for all and all for each. Wherever you take hold to help in these affairs, you will work with some one in a common cause; you will work, not for yourself alone, but for your country; not for your country alone, but for France, for England, for Belgium, for Serbia, for Russia, for Poland, for Italy, for Japan, for China, for all the world, to save it from the ruin of misapplied knowledge and selfish counsels. Nothing like this vast coöperation was ever known before. It used to be said that the United States had learned to think in the terms of a continent, and that Europe had got to learn that lesson. But now people must think in terms of all the continents. Nothing less than the whole world is in the pangs of readjustment; of hardly less than the whole world will you be a citizen when this work is finished.

But as you will remain distinctively a citizen of the United States, so, whatever you find to do, you will remain distinctively a woman. No extension of opportunity or novelty of occupation is going to swerve you from that inexorable condition. The work that you are to do in the world is to be woman's work. It may be driving an aeroplane or a motor-car, or making munitions, or keeping cows or chickens, or raising cabbages, or folding bandages, or nursing, or teaching, or knitting socks, or organizing enterprises, but if you do it, you make woman's work of it, for you are more important and less changeable than any occupation, and you will dominate the work, and not the work you.

If the work does not suit you as a woman, you will drop it presently, because it is more important in the long run that you should be a woman and do a woman's work than that any specified job should continue to be done. In an emergency, to be sure, the specific job may be all-important because the continuance of women's true work depends on it. But that is a temporary matter, to be cured at the first chance, so that the world may not cease to be worth living in, or run out of people.

I observe, and you will notice, that notwithstanding the great incursion of women, of late years, into one or another department of business, they are not of much account as fortune-builders. Some of them earn or make a good deal of money, but they seldom get rich by their own exertions, and nearly all the rich women have inherited their fortunes from men. Moreover, the women who are most successful as money-makers are not, as a rule, the most successful as women. The women seem to be a consecrated sex, too valuable to be employed in mere money-getting. Vast numbers of them earn a living — sometimes a good one — and have to; but few of them get rich. It is common for a young man to start out deliberately to accumulate a fortune. It is very uncommon for a young woman to do so. She is much more likely to accumulate a young man.

Atlantic Classics

Will you please take note of that, my daughter? In spite of your cap and gown, you are still a consecrated vessel, designed rather to confer benefits upon the world, than exact an excessive recompense for living in it. If you are to have much money you must get it indirectly. Your life is too valuable to be sacrificed to getting rich. I believe you will feel that to be true, no matter what you undertake; feel that you cannot afford to give up being a woman and fulfilling a woman's destiny, for the sake of winning the common rewards that are open to men. For you know man's great reward is woman. She is the crown of his endeavors and often the goal of them, but not of yours.

One of the consolations of these extraordinary times, so terrible and so afflicting in many aspects, is that they are bringing us closer to the French, the people in our modern world who seem to know best how to live, and who, we suspect, have come the nearest to solving the problem of the woman's place in life. Of course they are not a perfect model for us, and of course there are things that they may learn of us as well as we of them; but the Frenchwoman's place in life, as we hear of it, seems the nearest right that any people has worked out. It is a place of power and honor, a place in which the woman is valued to the full as a woman, and in which she coöperates intimately and effectively with the man. Probably we idealize the Frenchwoman's position somewhat, but as we see her, she is not only

A Father to his Graduate Girl

the decoration of life, but ideally the helpmate of the man; helping with her head and with her hands, with her companionship, her love, her thrift, her skill, her labor. We hear of her potency in business affairs; of her share, at least equal, and apt to be superior, in the management of farm and shop and household. We have learned all over again these last three years what wonderful stuff there is in the French, and wish there was more of it in the world. Never was mankind so much disposed to go to school to France, nor ever had this French tradition of woman's power and place and work a better chance to influence mankind. Perhaps it will help to temper in this land and generation the propensity to make a battle cry of 'Women for women,' with a prospect that it will yield in its turn to the slogan, 'Every woman for herself!'

Not with any such motto, my daughter, will civilization go any gait but backwards. The women of France have won great honor by great service, but their work has been woman's work. They have kept their hands on the details — the things that make the difference between profit and loss in trade or agriculture, and between paths of pleasantness and bad going in our daily walk. They are wise in the technique of living — not for themselves alone, but for France, her men and her children.

If France is pleasant and Frenchmen love it, it is Frenchwomen who have made it so. If life is pleasant to French men and they love it, it is French women who have made it so. If French men love France more than life, it is because in a conquered France, French life could not flourish, or French women train it and make it worth living to French men. It is a great office to make life pleasant; to make it worth living. So far as it is done, it is done chiefly by women, but not by women whose motto is 'Women for women,' or 'Every woman for herself.'

It is the fault of people who are good at details that they are prone to make details overshadow life. Perhaps the Frenchwomen have room among their virtues for that fault. It is one, my daughter, that your college education should help to keep you out of. I don't suppose that college has made you proficient in the details of life, but at least it should have qualified you to see the forest in spite of the trees. You ought in the end — and long before the end — to see life broader and truer for having been to college; and because of those three years of reading and listening and thinking, should be able to bestow your mind upon the details of life with less risk of their absorbing you.

But the best thing to save the spirit from being swamped by details is religion, which keeps the imagination alive and constantly reminds the hands and the brain what their activities are about. Most of the French women are religious, and that helps immensely to humanize them and keep them pleasant in spite of

A Father to his Graduate Girl

their strong bent toward thrift. Perhaps after the war France will offer the world a new-style Christian church, a church of France — Catholic as France is Catholic, free as France is free. Something like that is coming to all the world, and coming, sooner or later, out of the great dissolution of obstacles to human unity that is the great fruit and consequence of the war.

The wonderful war! The wonderful war! Praise God that we are in it, and practicing to beat the Devil along with our brethren! Be confident, my child, in the destiny of mankind! Here you come with that innocent sheepskin into a world loaded with new debts, mourning its innumerable dead, grieved at the havoc done to it, filled with orphans and widows and still struggling toward a goal obscured by smoke. But it is a world of promise beyond all the promise of a thousand years, in which whoever is strong in the faith may hope everything that saints foresaw or martyrs died to bring. Be glad it is your year. 'A.B. 1917' is distinction in itself. Accept it, my daughter, and make it good!

Printed by Libri Plureos GmbH in Hamburg, Germany